Learn Speed-Reading Fast

A Practical Guide on How to Read Faster,
Remember More, and Unlock Your Potential

Joseph Milano

Skill Builders

CONTENTS

Introduction

Much like anything worth having in this life, the ability to speed read successfully will come with time. In my opinion, true speed-reading is not the same as "skimming" as some may lead you to believe, where the information that you take in only stays in your memory for a few seconds before it flutters away. Speed-reading, when perfected, is a wonderful way to improve the quantity of what you read while retaining the quality too. Throughout this book, I will teach you the techniques, exercises and tips that you need to perfect your reading to a point where any of those huge books on your shelf, which have looked so intimidating for the last few years, will suddenly start looking more like a pleasant stroll rather than a trek up Everest!

Struggling with reading is a real and serious issue for a lot more people than you might think. Many of us, myself included, who have struggled or are still struggling with reading at a pace that we deem acceptable, can feel an undeserved sense of shame for our whole lives. This is not a healthy emotion to have hanging over us, and the way to overcome it is a much easier journey than you ever imagined, but it will take work.

Having trouble reading at a high level can stem from many sources. Having a teacher in our youth who just didn't understand, the wrong book and style choice early on, or some deep-rooted issue. Whatever the case may be, it is nearly always fixable, and before you know it, you will be reading at such a productive level that you will not only surprise yourself but everyone around you.

One of the myths surrounding speed-reading is that the information is not being processed in an acceptable manner. This is only really true of the aforementioned "skimming" and the two should never be confused. Don't get me wrong, skimming does have its uses, for example it can be effectively utilized to scan through a document for particular keywords, but as far as truly absorbing information goes, whether it be leaning from a self-help book or enjoying a story, I don't believe it to be a strong technique.

My own story (which we will go into in more detail in the first chapter) begins with a high school kid who could barely get through a sentence without breaking down, to student who could read through books at a rate of knots, with every bit of information being taken in and sticking.

Of course, books containing lots of specific technical information such as medical texts and technological works will always be slightly harder to ingest successfully compared to fiction, but they too can be massively improved with the training and exercises that we will discuss. So, if it is this sort of content that you are struggling with, do not be disheartened, as the reading of *all* literature styles can be improved through practicing speed-reading in the 'right way'.

Having studied endless texts (quickly!) on the subject of speed-reading, and having beaten my own struggles of the past comprehensively, I feel that I am in a strong position to point you in the direction of better and more pleasurable reading in the future.

We live in such a fast-paced world that it seems information is constantly being thrown in our faces. Learning how to process it in a quick and effective way can help us to rise above the pack and, more importantly to our well-being, not become overwhelmed. With social media and the likes of Wikipedia available at the swipe of a screen, having knowledge that we have learned and retained ready to go at an instant is a necessity now.

Once you have perfected your speed-reading skills, you will learn to banish the issues with reading that have held you back for so long. Slow progression, information not sticking, endless hours of studying, daydreaming and all of the problems that have previously been a thorn in your side will become a thing of the past. The sense of accomplishment that you will feel when you pick up a book and finish it in one sitting for the first time will be something that will stay with you forever. I can fully understand if this seems like an unattainable goal, but do not give up, as I've been there and I am here to help you on your journey.

From the first time that you count your words per minute (WPM) and begin to practice against your original time, you will see results early on. They won't be drastic at the start, of course, but they will be there. Once you can see tangible improvements, it will give you the strength and motivation to really dig into your training. I cannot promise that you will become the fastest reader in the history of literature, but what I *can* promise is that I will purely focus on teaching you the techniques that have been proven to be the most effective (and have helped me personally) to drastically improve your reading ability in a very short amount of time.

Together we will learn to cut out all distractions, improve focus and truly "get lost" in a book. Some of these tips and tricks you may have heard before, but when they are laid out in a straightforward way and explained by someone who has been where you are now, then practicing and perfecting them becomes a whole lot easier. You just need to stick with me until the end, and you will be well on your way.

As someone who was once where you are now, I know how you feel. Take it from a person who has made speed-reading a major part of their lives, once learned it's a skill that continues to grow and improve each and every time that it is used, and once the techniques are committed to memory and practiced daily, the whole process starts to feel easy. So, practice and patience are key. I can promise that through following the teachings in this book, you will become the type of reader that you always wanted to be.

Now, you may already be a competent reader, and you wish only to improve the decent standard that you already possess. This is admirable and bettering yourself with continued learning is an incredibly strong mindset to have. Luckily, the tips in this book are tried and tested and have already helped thousands of my clients (as well as myself) achieve some pretty outstanding results!

Seeing this book out until the end will take the people who really struggle with reading, and regular readers alike, to new and improved heights.

So, sit back and let me show you what I have learned over the years. It will be given to you in a conversational yet informative manner, so you will not feel overwhelmed or bogged down, and before you know it, *War and Peace* will seem like a walk in the park.

Chapter 1

The Start of the Journey

If you are reading this book, then at some stage in your younger years, you may have been in a similar position to where I began: Standing in front of a classroom of your friends and peers, sweating, shaking, and nervously holding a book. Those days when we were asked to read to the class were some of the most terrifying moments of our childhood, as not only a fear that we would humiliate ourselves descended upon us but a certainty, as well.

For me, it was William Golding's classic, *Lord of the Flies*. I was 13, and the teacher who, innocently enough I might add, asked me to read, was my English teacher the wonderful Mrs. Taylor. Although I was a good student—math and science were more my thing—she saw that my struggles with reading were not through a lack of application but through something more complex.

I vividly remember her keeping me after class one day, and out of earshot of the rest of the students, she asked me why I didn't try as hard with my English as I did with other subjects. I explained nervously that I really did want to do well in all of my studies, but I just couldn't grasp this particular one because of my incredibly low reading level. When she explained to me in a calm and reassuring manner that reading in front of the class would be no more until I felt ready, it was like the world's biggest weight had been lifted off my shoulders.

When I think back now, she must have spoken to the other teachers because reading in front of my friends ceased for me in all other classes, too, which gave me a chance to regroup and catch my breath. Her confidence in me and her reassurance that I was far from alone allowed me to realize that if this was the case, and other people had overcome, then I could, too.

Over time, as I began to stand in front of my math class and answer questions, or in front of the science students and explain the answer to a problem, she quickly figured out that it wasn't a matter of effort that was holding me back but the way in which my brain processed written information. Once we shifted my focus and I began to look out how the words could be consumed in a different, more suitable way, I rapidly became one of the strongest readers in the class.

As my love for reading, something that I had dreaded in my early years, became a burning passion, being one of the strongest readers amongst my peers just wasn't enough. Instead, I wanted to be able to devour literature in a way that would seem almost impossible to others; however, it was and is possible, and as I began to study the methods of speed-reading, I started to find a way to constantly improve not only the number of books I read but also my ability to retain more and more information.

Some of the tips and tricks I learned were utter trash, and I have disposed of them as quickly as I found them, leaving me with the tried and tested tactics that have worked so well for me and countless others. These are the select few that I will lay down in this book for you, so you will not only reap the benefits of everything that I have learned, but you will not have to go through the effort of separating the wheat from the chaff as I did. It has been done for you!

Before We Begin

Before we begin your speed-reading journey, let me just tell you this. A good, average words per minute range (WPM) is around 250. I am currently reading (many books, I might add) at 500 WPM. This may seem outrageous, but it is just a fact. It didn't flick on like a light switch (that would have saved a lot of time); I had to work hard. That being said, I did see the beginnings of results almost instantly.

Let me just put it into perspective a little more. The truth is that I struggled with even basic words through most of my childhood, and it wasn't until I got into my early teens that I could read fully. However, I still massively struggled. So, when we think of 500 WPM, we must add in the factor that I wasn't even starting on a level playing field to the other students. I had to come from behind to get the win, and you can too, regardless of where you perceive your current standard to be.

How good would it be to increase your average quality reading pace by 200 or 300%? Some people who practice the techniques that we will soon discuss have, like myself, gotten as high as a 500% improvement. Again, these numbers can seem staggering but only to someone who has never opened their mind fully to the huge self-improvement opportunities of speed-reading. By purchasing this book, you have clearly done so.

What speed-reading essentially does is open up your life up to everything else that is important to you. How? By freeing up your time. It is as simple as that. As we previously mentioned, today's life is just one big onslaught of information. If we do not learn how and what we need to process, then we are always in danger of being washed away by it. When we learn to process it quickly, we will not only take in exactly what we need to better our lives but will also do it in such a way that it will become second nature.

Imagine how effective study would become if you could read the material several times through and it only took about half the time, and everything stuck. Let yourself think about how pleasurable it would be to hand that book that your friend lent you back to them two days later and then discuss the wonderful story with them. Seeing their looks of amazement at how you read it so fast will always make you feel good, and the real thrill is that you got to enjoy a really good book without it driving you mad.

In a *Sage Journals* article from 2016, they refer to an amazing story about six-time World Speed-Reading Champion Anne Jones, who, in a bookstore in London, sat down and read a full Harry Potter novel in just under 48 minutes, which works out at around 4,200 WPM (Rayner et al.,, 2016).

Now, the skeptics would say that she could only have skimmed the book, but Miss Jones then proceeded to summarize the book for all of the journalists that were in attendance. How she did this remains knowledge to her and her alone, but you can guarantee that she did not learn this skill by accident. She took an already existing talent and honed it through practice.

The rest of us mere mortals do not necessarily have to aim for Anne Jones' levels of reading—that would take a lifetime for most of us. However, reaching levels that will surpass the majority can be very easily achieved through practicing the steps and exercises that we will lay down in this book.

Here are the main topics that I will explain for you:

- ▸▸ Calculate your WPM
- ▸▸ Meta guiding technique (tracking and pacing)
- ▸▸ Perpetual Expansion
- ▸▸ Evaluate your progress
- ▸▸ Learn to take it all in so the information sticks

There will of course be other little tips and tricks along the way, as well as some inspirational tones to help you maintain your journey, but these techniques listed above will be the basis of your training to become the speed-reader that you have always dreamt about.

When we read slowly, there is actually more chance of what we are reading being forgotten. This may seem strange, given that we would be led to believe that we are concentrating more, but it is actually the opposite. When we are "taking our time," we are only leaving ourselves open to more outside distractions.

If we are fully engrossed in a book, we will naturally pick up the pace of our reading as the story takes us. It is only when the material is boring us that we slow down. When we begin to hone our speed-reading skills and the information starts to get devoured, everything else around us fades away. "Getting in the zone" will become a habit, and when we boil speed-reading down, that is what we are left with.

While we perfect our speed-reading skills, our comprehension of the text naturally moves along with it. By this, I mean that no matter how quick your reading becomes, the information you are ingesting will remain with you long after the book or article is finished. At the end of the day, this is why we read. Even when it is just a romance novel or a James Patterson book, we still want to remember the plot and how the story ended, don't we?

Moving at a solid pace eliminates "back-skipping" too. When we slow our intake of the text down and those outside distractions start to play a part, oftentimes the words that we are reading become nothing but a side story. This is why thoughts of what we are going to make for dinner or the last episode of the show we watched the night before on Netflix take over. It is one of the most common problems related to issues pertaining to study, when the text that is being read is quite literally going in and slipping straight back out again.

When this occurs, it is almost always down to the pace at which it is being read. The most detrimental thing about this is that we are told to slow down and take our time when this happens. By the time you get to the end of this book and your WPM has gradually improved, you may feel a little peeved that what you have been told all along was seriously damaging any real chance that you had of learning how to take information in. In fact, it was making the whole process go backwards.

In the article previously mentioned, they separate reading into three different categories: reading, speed-reading, and skimming (Rayner et al., 2016).

Reading is of course the process of looking at text and absorbing as much or as little as the author allows through their style of writing and context. This is the most common way of taking in information, and it is perfectly fine for your average reader. The main issue with it is that there is little to no leg room provided for someone who is struggling with reading or for anyone who doesn't want to settle for average.

The beauty of speed-reading is that it can be learned and perfected by any level of reader if they put the time in. Whereas basic reading will have small variants in how much information goes in and the quickness this is achieved from person to person, speed-reading allows its students to race away from the pack to a far superior level. This is not meant in a condescending way, it is only to show that there are other levels and that they *can* be reached.

Although basic reading is fine for most, there are those of us that want more. Not only that, there are others, much like myself, who need to learn the gifts of speed-reading to get off the ground floor. When we learn that struggling with words at an early age—and even later in life, if it was never addressed—is nothing to be ashamed of, we can then pinpoint the problem and start to do something about it.

Skimming, as we briefly touched on, is when we literally skim through a text for a certain section or word. This is more of a research tool; as the digital age becomes more and more advanced, it is beginning to fade, but it will still always exist as far as hard copies of novels and study papers are concerned. A common time that it will happen to us is when we do the dreaded "zone out" during a book that we are reading and realize after 20 minutes that we haven't absorbed anything for the whole last chapter.

But as we now know, this will cease being a problem once we learn how to improve our WPM and our attention becomes laser-focused on whatever we read. When this begins to become part of our lives, skimming will become a thing of our past.

Speed-reading surpasses both of these. This is just how it is and not the bold statement that it may seem. When we learn to take in all the information we can and at a much faster rate, then it can only be superior, can't it?

This journey that you are about to embark on will change how you view books and study in general forever. No more will the shelf where they reside fill you with dread as you count the amount of them that you started and never finished. It will only make you feel excitement as each of them becomes "something else that you have read" over a very short period.

Reading and the quest for knowledge are some of the most fundamental things in bettering ourselves and in finding an escape from the frantic world around us. Educational texts allow us to climb higher in life as we learn and become a more intellectual version of ourselves.

Novels and stories are what excite us and fill us with a joy that nothing else can. When struggles with comprehension or time restraints take these things away from us, we can let a little part of ourselves remain lost.

Speed-reading allows us to sharpen our tools. It gives us the gifts of literature and learning, and it does so with all of the keys available in a rapid and productive manner. When you start to see the positives of what I have to teach, you will wonder how you ever got by without it; as the realization that your struggle with reading cannot only be fixed but perfected, you will find yourself in a whole other world that you had previously presumed was too far away.

I am going to show you some of the simple, yet lifesaving methods that Mrs. Taylor showed me. If you were, or are, that scared child shaking like a leaf in front of a class of onlookers, then they will help you in the way that they helped me. All of the things I have learned along the way will be here, too. Much like any skill in life, they take practice, but the payoff will be more than a fair trade. Maybe someone you know is struggling with the same thing, and you will know how to help them through it. We are all in this together.

By practicing the techniques in these pages, everything that you thought about the struggles of reading will soon be banished to the past. Just by practicing each of them a little every day, the results will come very early on. Once this happens, the rest will accelerate, and before you know it, you will unlock your full reading ability.

In the following chapters, I will give you the guidance that you need to unlock your potential. I will pass on everything that I have learned. There will be no judgment (I was there too, remember) and there will be no fluff, only one person holding out his hand in the hope that you take it. My goal is to show you that the very thing that you thought was impossible or perhaps even a bit scary, is in truth, just what you always wanted.

Chapter 2

The First Test:

Calculate Your Current Reading Speed

In this chapter, we will find out what our baseline speed is in WPM. The purpose of this is not to make us feel bad when the results come in, or we think that it is well below average or not what we had imagined it to be. All we are doing is giving ourselves a foundation to build our speed-reading on. Once we have this, we can compare the guaranteed improvements to our old score and begin to feel better about our progression almost instantly.

Now, do not be disheartened if the numbers are low, that is why we are here. As we stated at the beginning of the book, a decent average is around the 250 WPM mark, so whether you are well below or are hitting these types of numbers, then there is always room for improvement, and we all want that.

It is of vital importance that your baseline is calculated accurately. There is no point in padding the answer to make you feel better, as this will skew how much you have improved when you recalculate you WPM in the future. Once you have worked out your baseline correctly, although it may seem like a small job, it's an incredibly important step to seeing your speed-reading and reading efficiency grow; the first step towards achieving any goal in life is always the most crucial.

As soon as you have your baseline sorted, you can grab a fresh pad of paper and write it at the top. Do not be worried about the number there because you are going to be so far ahead of that score soon that it will be nothing but a memory. So, write that number down with pride, as it is confirmation that you are ready to take this thing on and win.

The importance of an honest baseline is not only to let you see the improvements as you go along, it is like a landmark for yourself, as starting something on the wrong foot will only lead to you tripping up; anything that demotivates or stops you in your progression will not be good.

We are now coming up to your baseline test. To do this, you will need to make sure that you take some time alone to do it. There is no point in trying to do it in the cafeteria at work or on public transport, as the distractions of the people and things around you will be far too present. What you need to do is wait until the kids are in bed or the game on the TV is over and set yourself up comfortably. This is not to say that you will need to do this every time that you want to read, far from it—this will only be at the beginning so you can get an accurate number.

You *could* just count all the words you are about to read one by one and figure out how many you have done per minute that way, but this is all about improving your speed, not how to partake in mundane tasks. The formula below will always work out better in the long run anyhow, as books vary in word space, size, and style. Essentially, we are getting an average that will apply to all literature, not just the particular novel that we have chosen for the test.

Of course, when it comes to reading—and anything else that takes concentration—there will be days when the going is a little tougher. This can be caused by any number of things like tiredness, distraction, things on our mind, or even the book just not being that great. The key is to power through. If the book is just a terrible book, then switch it out for the test, but try not to get into this habit too often, as it can become a reason for us to give up on our journey, which would just be wasted time.

Try to always remember why you are doing this—to get to a level of reading that is not only better than where you were but better than most. This will help you to stay the course. Everyone that is here now wants to improve their WPM, and if you see this thing out, then it will happen. Practice is the only way to perfection.

Here are the steps you will need to follow to find out your baseline speed. Remember to read at your normal pace when doing this test. Do not try to overdo it and prove a point. The idea is to find out how quickly you read right now:

- Select a passage from a book that you have never read before

- Calculate how many words per line you have (count the words in five lines, then divide it by five)

- Start a three-minute timer on your phone

- Read at your usual pace

- Stop when time is up

- Count how many lines you read and multiply this by the average words per line

- Divide this answer by three (the three minutes)

- There you have it: your current reading speed (baseline)

If your initial score is low, please don't fret, as it is only a marker; it is just there to mark your future scores against. You need it to assess where you are and where you want to be. All that matters from here on out is the scores you write below it as they gradually improve. Remember what Paul Chek said, "If you're not assessing, then you're guessing." I think we can all understand how important it is to keep a record of how we are progressing (Masters Fitness, 2016).

Speed-reading has been around for a lot longer than we may think, and since Evelyn Wood first coined the phrase in the 50s, it has been improved upon and tinkered with for 70 years ("Evelyn Wood (teacher)," 2020). This has resulted in these tried and tested methods that I am laying out for you here, and through the decades of filtering, you will be left with only the best.

As we mentioned earlier, the type of text you choose will result in a different WPM. This is the same for anyone, so if you have chosen James Joyce's *Ulysses* over say, George Orwell's *Animal Farm*, then you will get different results. This is only because the difference in narration and prose in both books is quite vast. Both wonderful novels of course, and by two of the greatest authors who ever lived, but *Ulysses* is a tough read for anyone. Starting on a book like this, especially when the main goal at the beginning is just to improve ourselves, is likely to be counterproductive.

Although you are choosing a book that you have never read before, try and at least choose one in a genre that you enjoy. That way, it will seem a lot less like a tedious exercise than the enjoyable, yet highly productive, experience that it is. If medical books or academic journals are where you want to get to, do not worry, as the speed-reading you learn will apply to all texts in time.

Once you have all distractions taken care of, and you have calculated your baseline, then you are done for that day. Just a few minutes work, sure, but this is something that you will need to practice *every* day, so we do not want to overload you at the start. Now, this is just your training that I am talking about. It is important for you to keep reading on through the next chapter while it is all still fresh in your mind, but if you feel a little overwhelmed, then you should take a breather. Getting your WPM average down on paper is enough for the beginning, as tomorrow you will be straight back at it, and I know that you are going to crush it.

We will of course be going through the other techniques that we listed in the first chapter, and as you get through each chapter from here on out, you will quickly see the changes occurring. All of these techniques will be delivered to you in much the same way as we have been doing—relaxed and helpful—but if you keep the practice up, they will get you to where you want to be.

Now that you have your initial WPM reading sorted, you are ready to start getting really stuck in your speed-reading. In the next chapter, we are going to step it up a notch by discussing the wonderful tried and tested Meta Guiding Technique, where we will delve into the history of it all and bring to light its numerous proven benefits. Keep on reading, and pin your first baseline calculations up on the refrigerator if you want to. Soon, you will see such a drastic change in how you devour books that you may want a reminder of how far you have come from time to time.

Chapter 3

Slow is Smooth, Smooth is Fast
The Meta Guiding Technique

When Evelyn Wood (1909–1995) started making waves with her revolutionary take on speed-reading in the 50s, she never could have imagined how quickly it would take off. Of course, she would have known that a need to consume information at a much quicker rate would be fundamental if perfected, especially in a world where the Internet was not available, but as her business spread and endorsements from the likes of John F. Kennedy began to surface in the media, the thing that she was trying to teach became national news. As millions of people began to improve themselves through the powers of speed-reading, her name was forever etched in the history of the printed word.

Speed-reading, or as Mrs. Wood called it, "dynamic reading," would go from a small family-run dream business to over 180 schoolrooms across the United States and Canada in a few short years. This was helped by a glowing article in *Time* magazine, and after her years of teaching pupils and studying how they and her peers read, she began her journey of improving her and the world's WPM ("Evelyn Wood (teacher)," 2020).

The basis of what she taught still runs through speed-reading today, with a few tweaks and improvements along the way. Reading down the page, rather than side to side, reading groups of words or complete thoughts, never rereading, and eliminating subvocalization (mouthing the words or reading under one's breath) all remain today. However, with my improvements and delivery, we can now help your reading even more than when the great Evelyn Wood first introduced speed-reading.

You have already gotten your baseline in the previous chapter, but that does not mean that you are done—far from it. There is still a lot of work to do, and we can only get to where we want to be through time and effort. Although there are still a few techniques to come, they will all be laid out in an easy-to-follow and helpful way, so just keep doing what you are doing, as you are doing great so far.

I understand more than most the pains of struggling with reading, and this is why I have written this book. Together, we will get you to the levels that you require and much, much further. If you have gotten this far, then the rest is there for the taking. It is just a matter of application and determination.

In this chapter, we are going to look at the Meta Guiding Technique. This involves taking a playing card, a pen, or even your finger, and covering the lines to come in each paragraph as you read. We will not be running the card (or whatever you choose) along each word as we did with our finger in school when we first learned to read. But the principle is the same.

This time, instead of each word, we will use the card for each line. What we need to do is move the card (or marker) at a certain pace, almost independently from our reading. The idea is not to move the card as we finish each line but more so to try and keep our reading up with the movement. This may seem a little difficult at first, as all of our training in reading from school and after, involves us allowing our own, slower pace to dictate how fast we read.

How quickly we move the marker down the page will become a habit after a while, and as it does, the speed will naturally increase as we improve. What you need to remember is that practice is the only way to see these improvements, and if an urge to throw in the towel early tries to pull at your sleeve, just remind yourself of your goal and push on. Keep the marker moving at a constant speed, regardless of how slow you think it is at first. It will improve.

The first few times you try this, you may even let the comprehension of the text become secondary, for now. All we are trying to do is get your rhythm settled and your speed at a comfortable level. Try to read something that you think you will enjoy, sure, but try and remember that the first book or two are only training, so do not try to go back if you think you missed something while reading. You can always plow through the book a second time when your speed-reading has sufficiently improved.

You will be going back over the same paragraph at first, but this is only early on (the steps later in the chapter will explain this in more detail), as we are more concerned with getting a set speed.

As a general rule, rereading is always a big no-no in speed-reading. This is because it is always counterproductive. Even for regular readers, going back over something that they presumed they have missed normally turns out to be nothing, as what they thought they had passed over is actually explained later on. The reason that they zoned out was because they were reading too slowly, or they were distracted. As we know from the earlier chapters, when you implement the techniques of speed-reading and they begin to manifest themselves in your subconscious, things like distractions and rereading become a distant memory.

The only time that we allow you to go back over text is during practice, and that is only to get your rhythm with the marker up to scratch, as that is the most important thing with this technique. I know this may seem a little tedious at first, but it is of vital importance to perfect it, so remember to concentrate and work hard.

Using a marker to block out what is coming in the book is also a wonderful tool for people who have ADHD, as the constant need to skip forward and backward for fear of missing something starts to be eliminated. When we are only concentrating on each line rather than every individual word, we are able to immerse ourselves in the story being told or the information that we need to ingest.

Take this sentence:

"Alan felt that he couldn't take it anymore."

Pretty basic, right? Now, let me show you how the average person processes this sentence without even knowing they are doing so.

1. Alan
2. Alan felt
3. Alan felt that
4. Alan felt that he
5. Alan felt that he couldn't
6. Alan felt that he couldn't take
7. Alan felt that he couldn't take it
8. Alan felt that he couldn't take it anymore.

This happens because we are brought up to process every word as one single entity, so when we read a sentence, it is not taken in as one whole piece of information but single words that we have to constantly link. Our subconscious has to keep adding the next word in as we go until the sentence is complete.

When we think of written a language such as Mandarin, quite often whole words will be represented with one symbol. The information that they receive from a symbol that is basically one letter to the English-speaking world still processes as the word it represents. No information is lost by this—it only takes less time. When we begin to take words as the singular entity that they are, we can start to let the information they represent into our subconscious at a much faster rate. It is how we perceive the structure that affects our intake.

Once the words become what they really are, then the same will begin to happen with sentences, as each word in it will be processed as one whole piece of information. This will of course take more practice as time goes on, but for people such as myself who read at a 500 WPM plus rate with full comprehension, the payoff far outweighs the effort—yours will, too.

Here is the sentence again in another format. You will see that the structure of the letters is not important, it is only how we process them:

"Alan flet taht he cuodlnt tkae it aynmroe."

Now, this may read like gibberish at first glance, but we still understand it. Not only that, the information will be processed at the same rate as if it was spelled correctly, much as it had been previously. This is not to be taken as part of the exercise, it is only to show that our subconscious and our ability to take in information is a lot more open and untapped than we sometimes give ourselves credit for.

The Meta Guiding Technique works so well for a number of reasons, but one of the main ones is "chunking." This is when we learn to take large chunks of information in one go and eliminate the subvocalizing that we previously touched on, which will be touched on later! As the marker unveils each new line, we will begin to process each sentence as a whole, which will again improve over WPM.

After a time, your subconscious will instinctively know what "keywords" are in a sentence. Copula verbs (or linking verbs) such as, am, is, are, seem, and many more will just become part of the sentence as a whole. They are important, of course, as all words are, but they will just be processed in a different way as your practice takes hold.

A lot of the fear surrounding speed-reading as a whole is that information will be missed or lost along the way. This is always a risk when you *skim* the page, as we touched on earlier. However, when you have perfected these techniques in their truest form, you will start to see that not only is the information going in but that it is staying around for a lot longer than before. As we know, speed-reading is a lot different to skimming.

Some of the later techniques that you learn will allow you to close in your peripherals on the page and lock in the information that we need to process the whole paragraph and to take it all in as a whole, but that is for later. Right now, we are concentrating on just getting your tracking up to speed, so to speak.

In my opinion, the most detrimental cause of slow reading is "back-skipping." By this, I mean a constant need to look back over what we have read, through fear of having missed some vital information, through our mind wandering, or for many other reasons, as well. Regardless of which one, they all have the same effect. Once we eliminate this hindrance, we can begin to take reading for what it really is: an essential part of who we are as human beings. If we cannot only perfect it, but move past this level a few hundred percent, then we are well on our way to bettering ourselves in something that we have previously had a love/hate relationship with.

When we bring a marker into the equation and our only concentration is on the sentences that we are processing, and we learn to make the secondary movement of the object we are marking with to fade into the background, then the Meta Guiding Technique quickly becomes part of our speed-reading arsenal. It is one of our most important weapons, and although it may feel a little awkward at first, as your WPM improves and you begin to master the added comprehension, it will all fall into place with practice.

Before we begin our training, let me just reiterate the point that the information you are about to take in does not need to stick for now. All we are doing here is improving your technique and smooth eye tracking, so do not beat yourself up too much if you miss a few names here and there.

Here is what you need to do.

- Get a marker (a card is best, but a pen or finger will suffice).

- Set a timer for three minutes.

- Place it directly under the first line, flat across the page.

- With your dominant hand, find a pace that is at your normal reading speed and begin to move the card down a line as you finish the first sentence. I find that using a card works well to help you to track and pace smoothly though the text.

- As soon as you are finished with the paragraph, go back, and try to improve your speed—you will want to be doing each line in one second early on in the process.

- Do not worry about comprehension just yet.

- Try to gradually eliminate the thoughts of movement and concentrate on the reading aspect and the movement.

- Relax your eyes and allow them to absorb the words as they track across them.

- Mark your results.

- Take a minute break and repeat the process, but try to do a line in half a second.

The idea of your first few attempts is only to get a rhythm. The comprehension and quality of what you are reading are not really that important just yet. Some will not even take *any* information at all in the first few times, and that is okay for now. What you need to do is keep marking down your time and stick with it. Once you begin to eliminate distractions like looking ahead to see what happens in the next paragraph, your focus and attention get locked into one single goal. That goal? Reading. Fast.

Another trick that I have personally introduced to my speed-reading, and it applies to the Meta Guiding Technique especially, is taking a moment at the end of each paragraph to flick my eyes up. This only takes a second and it gives your brain a chance on a neurological level to file away the information that you have just read. It will barely affect your time, but it will drastically improve your capacity to hold onto the information, and the positives of how it gets stored will be priceless. You do not have to look at anything in particular, just a flick of the eyes to let the information find its place.

Now that you have begun practicing this technique, you must continue to do so. Eliminating all distractions is a must because until you are fully experienced in all aspects of speed-reading, your full concentration will always be needed. As your progression in this technique improves, you will then be able to start letting in more of the information that is being consumed. If that is already happening, then great, and you can advance onto improving the rest. But for those of us who are only getting our tracking in shape, then we have to read, repeat, and read again.

In the next chapter, we will be discussing how to train your peripheral vision on the page you read. This, when added to the Meta Guiding Technique and the rest to follow, will work like a support system, as each lesson learned helps the other one along in the process. By reading this book and following the lessons that are being passed on, you are only doing yourself good, so keep on reading and don't stop practicing. You will thank me later!

Chapter 4

Perceptual Expansion
Training Your Peripheral Vision

This technique is such an important one, and although it will require plenty of practice, the results that you are aiming for will start to happen very early on. By eliminating a certain percentage of the words that we concentrate on (they still register, so don't worry), we instantly reduce the time that it takes to read a book. Although we are still reading the words, we are not physically moving our direct vision onto them, thus lowering the strain on our eyes at the same time as speeding up our consumption of the text.

Perceptual expansion is improving one's vision of what they see on the peripheral, or each side. There are only slight changes that you have to make physically; it is mostly a matter of acknowledging that you already possess this ability and letting that sink in. When you do this, you will already have a 66% advantage over regular readers, as your central vision will only be focusing on the 33% of the text that remains (Yu et al., 2018). Your peripheral will do the rest.

This may sound tough, but with the right training, this will become second nature. It is all in your perception, and when you learn to shake off some of the bad habits that most of us were brought up using and implement the ones you learn here, then you will begin to see that there is a much easier, more efficient way to read. The speed will come, and through training your peripheral vision, you will be certain to improve it drastically.

Our peripheral vision, as you probably know, is everything that you see on each side of what you are actually looking at. It is the part of your vision that alerts you of oncoming traffic when you are daydreaming and about to cross the street too early or if someone is coming up beside you at the watercooler at work. Often we take it for granted, as there aren't many times in life when we need to use it, or at least that's how we can feel. Yet, our peripheral vision is always in play, we just don't harness it as much as we should. Until now.

What we see out of the corner of our eyes is always being registered, even when we do not realize that it is. Things that we see during the day are stored away in our subconscious. Usually, the things that we recall when we are trying to remember them are everything that we have taken in through our centered vision, but events and objects that happened around us are constantly also being registered; it is just normally being processed almost independently.

When we become aware of our peripheral vision by, say, holding our hand out at arm's length in front of us and concentrating on one finger, we can begin to understand that we are also seeing objects on either side of it. The only difference is that we are not paying any attention to them, but as soon as we do, they are registered in our conscious mind, too.

This is the basic principle of perceptual expansion. All we are doing is becoming aware of our peripheral vision and using it to observe the words that we can push to the side as we read. This probably sounds more complicated than it is in reality, but I promise you that it is only a matter of accepting that the information is constantly going in and relaxing in this knowledge. Once you do this, your WPM will have grown drastically very early on, and all of this is guaranteed to improve as you practice this and the other techniques in this book, but for now, an almost instant improvement is still pretty impressive.

Saccadic eye movement is a whole different aspect. If you close one eye and lift an object up in front of your vision (a pen or anything small will do), you will be able to do a quick test on eye movement and begin to understand a bit of the science behind what we are doing here. Move the pen slowly from side to side and track it with your open eye. Once you start doing this, you will begin to notice that your vision does not move smoothly, but follows in more of a jerky movement. This is because our brain does not register images in a consistent, one-reel way. It is more like a camera phone on "burst mode," as we implant the things we see in our mind with little singular images.

In the second edition of the scientific text, *Neuroscience*, we learn that "Saccadic eye movements are said to be ballistic" because we are not able to register the constant changes we see in "the course of the eye movement" (Purves et al., 2016). This is not to say that the information isn't going in. All it means when applied to the intake of text is that the longer the line we read, then the more the eye will flick from one section of it to the next. When we close the peripheral lines in, we give ourselves less actual scanning to do, which not only helps with time and WPM, but it also gives our eyes a bit more of a break and eliminates tiredness and backtracking (Purves et al., 2016)

Take this excerpt paragraph as an example:

"Even when he had begun to play music at fourteen, he never would have guessed that it would come to this. His idol, his hero, the man that had made him pick up a guitar in the first place, was not only standing in the crowd but had given him a nod of acknowledgement. At least he thought that it was a pleasant nod. What if Frankie Fingers had actually meant it in a condescending way? He didn't want to think about that."

Now, when we read this in the way that we have all been brought up to do so, our eyes run along each word as we take in the information. If we begin to eliminate the peripheral words, we can start to ingest it as a whole. You will not need to draw the imaginary lines too far just yet, just a word or two in length on each side, depending on the size of each one. But as time progresses, you may begin to edge it in a little more until you get to a third of the text on both sides.

Let's try it again, but with the first word or two on each side eliminated from our eye movement. It will still register, only now your eye movement will start at the second or third word on every line and end on the second or third from last.

I've added some guidelines in the following example to help:

"Even when he had begun to play music at fourteen, he never would have guessed that it would come to this. His idol, his hero, the man that had made him pick up a guitar in the first place, was not only standing in the crowd but had given him a nod of acknowledgment. At least he thought that it was a pleasant nod. What if Frankie Fingers had actually meant it in a condescending way? He didn't want to think about that".

Do you see how it all registered? We are not ignoring the other words, this is only about not wasting our direct vision where we do not have to. Think of it like a boxer conserving his energy. It is a long fight, sure, but if they use their strengths where they are really effective, then they are not just burning themselves out, flailing wildly at thin air.

Implementing the steps to come a little later in this chapter, and repeating them until they stick is the only way to improve your perceptual expansion. Along with the Meta Guiding Technique (which you will need to keep using as you practice this), everything will start to combine. There are more tips and tricks to come, but much like what you have learned already, they will all click together as one essential technique.

If you feel the need to practice early on by drawing a physical line down each side of the page in an old book or a magazine, then feel free to do just that. Whatever helps you to get to where you want to be is all progress. Just be sure that it isn't a first edition!

Much like the Meta Guiding Technique that we have already been practicing, your comprehension is not a big factor here early on. Over time, it will be, of course, as that is why we are all here, but for now, just perfecting how you train your eye movement and understanding that the ballistic aspect of how they operate will be enough. When you have practiced a few times, you can start to concentrate on what is sticking and what isn't, but if you work hard, the comprehension will happen organically.

The human brain is a wonderful, complex thing. When we try and grasp the magnitude of what it can achieve for us, then we are already on a path to self-improvement. There are no major epiphanies needed here, just the understanding that we can allow our subconscious to work right alongside us. The information that it is taking in as we go about our day is always there. We just need to know how and when to access it.

If you have already been using a playing card as described earlier, then great. If not, then I recommend using one for this, as the length of it will basically come out to where you want your peripheral lines to be. A credit card will also work perfectly.

Let's begin the exercise:

- Set your timer for three minutes.

- Much like the example earlier, trace an imaginary (or physical if you feel the need) line down both sides of the page.

- Make sure to track and pace as we have already learned, keeping at a fast pace.

- Keep your central vision on the text inside the lines.

- When your time is up, take a minute and begin again.

Let's go through the technique and in more detail; now that you have your steps, you must begin to implement them. Do not be afraid to go back over the same text here. What we are doing is moving our borders in as we progress. As we get better each time, the goal is to automatically set them one-third of the way in on both sides. This will take time, so do not try and do it instantly. Stick to the one or two words (depending on size), and work on that for now.

Once you have your timer set, you can begin. Remember that if you need to draw an actual line down the page, then use an old book or something disposable. If you are still using a credit or playing card to track and pace, then the length should be sufficient.

As I have mentioned through the other chapters, your initial goal is only to improve the technique that you are practicing at first. Try not to be too hard on yourself if the information is not sticking at the beginning. This will come with time. All you need is patience and determination: I will supply you with the rest, but you do need to stick to it. Without your dedication to consistently practice and develop your skills, these techniques will be useless.

Remember to track and pace as you go. This is key, as letting the older techniques that you have learned slip will be extremely counterproductive and will only result in you having to go back over them again each time. This is akin to back-skipping on a much broader scale, and nobody wants that. The good news is that tracking and pacing are not only a vital part of training your perceptual expansion, but they will aid the progress, too.

The ultimate goal with each turn is to strengthen your peripheral vision. But remember that it is already there and that what you are doing is more so strengthening your awareness of it. When doing this, you will be tempted to move your direct vision to the first and last letters on the page. This is just a habit kicking in and you need to gradually eliminate this. Again, try not to beat yourself up too much when it does happen—because it will at first—just keep speed-reading until the alarm goes off, and start again: The results will come.

The wonderful Tim Ferriss tells us in his blog from 2009 that we must practice these techniques "at three times the speed of your ultimate target reading speed." This is to say that although you will be practicing at an initial speed that seems scary, you are only learning the actual movements and skills, not the comprehension. It is just a little nudge in the direction of accepting that these things take effort.

Each time that you have taken your minute break and started again, you will most probably start to notice instant improvements. This is just your perceptual expansion kicking into gear as the practice takes hold. Take these little wins and store them away each time; they are your way of knowing that what you are doing is working, and if you go again when that timer goes, it will be even more productive the next time.

Remember that even if you came into this with a decent average of around 250 WPM, through this technique—which is essentially eliminating two-thirds of the page—you will quickly see a drastic change in these numbers, and with solid dedicated practice, could reach as high as 750 WPM. Just try and comprehend that for a minute: Try and think of how quickly you will finish that book that has been staring at you from the shelf. A whole new world of how you devour literature is there for the taking.

If it is study that you struggle with and you are buried in educational textbooks, the general rule is not to try and read three times as many books once you have brought your WPM up but to read the same one quickly three times. The reason for this is that although you are spending roughly the same amount of time, you are ingesting the information an extra couple of times. This allows it to become firmly implanted in your memory, and isn't that the basis of all study?

Now that you have begun practicing your perceptual expansion technique, you can begin to combine it with your track and trace. Again, keep a note of your progress, as actually seeing the results and acknowledging them is a great morale booster. This will all be covered in the next chapter, as we take a much more detailed look at evaluating our progress and treating it much like any other exercise in our lives. By this, I mean that the more you do it, the better you will become.

Enjoy!

Chapter 5

Evaluate Your Progress

Now that you have practiced your techniques and you are starting to get the hang of things, it is time to evaluate your progress. Yes, I know, it seems early, but that is the beauty of learning to speed read; once you learn the simple yet extremely effective steps that I have shown you, everything else is just practicing them until you are at your desired WPM.

Your brain, which is just like a muscle, gets stronger the more you train it. If we do five sit-ups a day, we are not going to end up with a washboard stomach. However, if we set aside a good amount of time and regularly workout with a structured program, then soon enough, the picturesque abs that we always wanted will inevitably start to show themselves. This is not a trick, and much like speed-reading, if you put the time and work in, then the results will be guaranteed to follow.

Whenever we sit down to read, even before our lessons here, we will always feel that little initial buzz in our minds. Oftentimes, it takes a few pages until we really kick into gear, and this is especially prevalent when we haven't picked up a book in a while. This is just our mind and our eyes being out of practice, and when you are someone who struggles with reading at a pace that keeps you interested, this can be even harder to maintain.

The amazing thing about speed-reading is not only the number of books that you will be able to consume as your WPM improves but the love for literature that will come with it. If you have picked up this book, then there is a massive part of you that already feels this way, but it is only the tediousness of the actual process that has held you back. Now that you are ready to evaluate your progress, you are at a stage where the training will soon switch to comprehension. You still need to be patient, as there is some way to go in your progress; however, you are doing so well, and I am sure you will be reading at a level that will amaze you soon enough.

As we progress through the steps in this chapter, we will begin to test our comprehension, as that is the reason that we are all here, isn't it? What we all want is to not only get through that array of books that have piqued our interest over the years but to understand and remember everything that they have to offer. This will all come with practice, of course, and as we use the points that will be provided soon, the absorption of the text that you are using to practice will start to sink in.

Before we move to the next step, I am going to need you to take a moment and congratulate yourself on how well you are doing. This may seem silly at first, but anyone who takes a look at something in their lives and decides that it is not to their liking and they want to make a change deserves all of the plaudits that the world has to offer. It is not an easy thing to take that first step, and if you have gotten to this point in your training, then you are doing wonderful things, so you should be proud of yourself.

Speed-reading is not only about consuming a massive amount of books—it is also about *enjoying* them to their fullest. Some people, from the outside looking in, may believe that the only reason for learning such a valuable skill would only be for the use of students who have fallen a bit behind on their studies. This could not be further from the truth, and most of us who master these techniques, myself included, use them for the pleasure of reading as much as the intake of knowledge.

What you will need to do from here is set yourself up as you did when we found your original baseline in the second chapter, "The First Test." Only now you will be implementing all of the other techniques that you have learned thus far. The key here is to start to register your WPM with all of the previous steps put into practice together. What you will find is that once the peripheral expansion and the Meta Guiding Technique are used as one, then you will already see an improvement from your original baseline.

For testing comprehension, the trick is to read some text that you have never read before. Read at your new improved speed (faster if you can), and when you are finished, take a piece of paper, and write down four or five key points that you believe mattered to the plot or text. Once this is done, you can reread at a slower pace (not too slow!), making sure to take everything in. As you do this, you will need to take a mental note of how many important points you picked up, and how many you missed.

There will probably be points that you missed, but this is not a problem. You must remember that you likely to be scrutinizing yourself far more than you ever would when you are just reading casually. Even the most experienced readers will miss something here and there, so try and understand that we are only practicing right now: the real results will come.

When making a note of what you registered and what you didn't, you should only be viewing the results in one way— the points that you caught. Whatever we missed is secondary, as we are only learning, and every time that you do it, more and more will stick. I am not talking about when you go over the same text again. What I mean is, as the techniques and the training become part of who you are, then the comprehension will drastically improve.

Our brains need to be challenged and worked to improve or even to maintain their current standard. Your cognitive skills and memory function need constant engagement throughout your lifetime, and speed-reading not only ticks this box but also challenges them to improve drastically.

In a 2021 article in *Harvard Health Publishing*, Doctor John N. Morris of the Institute for Aging Research tells us that as far as your brain is concerned, "Practice makes permanent." He also tells us that, "You can't improve memory if you don't work at it. The more time that you devote to engaging your brain, the more it benefits" ("Train your brain," 2021).

These are things that we are all mostly aware of, but the brain itself and the endless strengths that it had can sometimes get overlooked in a world that through Instagram and Facebook, had become more about shaping and toning the body more so than the mind. When we understand that something we possess of such importance to our well-being can be trained by doing something like reading, then the possibilities are endless.

Think of speed-reading as swimming for the brain. Not only are you giving it the workout that it needs through some form of mental interaction, but you are working every part of it at once. Cognitive skills and thinking, in general, will be made to work, and the amazing thing is that you don't have to stress about how long it will take at the gym or how much of an effort it will be. All you are doing is reading, and that is a pleasurable experience for everyone.

Let's get into the steps you will need follow to evaluate the progress that you have made so far. The goal here is to use a combination of all the techniques we have been through together so far. I have laid everything out for you in order, which will make the process nice and easy to follow!

Find yourself a quite space as before, to make the test as accurate as possible.

Set yourself up as before, removing any distractions

Use a timer again. Give yourself five minutes this time so you can really get into it and cover a lot of points:

- Set your mental (or physical) borders on both sides of the page.

- Get your marker (pen, finger, or card) and set it at the start of the text.

- Read down through the text as quickly as you can. Do not stop or backtrack.

- When you are done, mark down a few of the main points in the text that stuck with you.

- Set everything else aside and reread the text carefully.

- When your five minutes are up, work out your new WPM.

- Check your comprehension by marking down the points in the text that stuck.

- Reread the text more carefully and compare the points you wrote down.

- Take a couple of minutes rest, and start again on a new page.

Remember that the comprehension will come, and if you have been stringent with your practice, then it will come to you much quicker. Just remain patient and continue to give yourself a pat on the back here and there. This may seem a little tough sometimes, but I can promise from my own experience that it really is worth the time and effort.

If you go back over the text and realize that you only noted one important point, do not be disheartened. The reason that you have decided to take this journey was that you were struggling with reading at a level that you desired, so any progress at this early stage is good progress—keep at it.

Always practice each of the techniques together until they have become second nature. Prioritizing one over the other will be counterproductive, and like any machine that runs smoothly, all of the parts need to be well oiled. As we stated before, each of the things that you practice will hold the other one up, and in turn, it will help with the training of the next one. You just need to take the rough with the smooth.

Taking negatives to heart with anything that we try in life often seems a lot easier than embracing the positives. This can apply to work, life, love, or any number of events and emotions that we experience. Learning an essential new skill like speed-reading is no different, and you need to learn how to stack up the wins in your progress as you achieve them and put the losses aside. Concentrating on the negatives will only lead to you becoming disheartened. Focus on your achievements, like how far you have come so far and the improvements that you are seeing every time you come back to practice.

The positive effects will come quickly though, so taking the rough with the smooth will be easily done. What you need to remember is to not give up if your WPM comes out low at first or your perceptual expansion stays at a one-word border for the first few days. This only means that you are trying to perfect your speed-reading, and there is nothing at all wrong with that.

If, on the other hand, you are getting superb results early on, then sticking with the training is just as important. The last thing you want is to become lackadaisical and allow your standards to drop. Of course, if your WPM and comprehension have improved drastically early on, then fair play to you, but there is always room for improvement, and you never know where it can take you in the end if you stick with it.

Britannica (2021) explains the Law of Diminishing Returns like this: "If one input in the production of a commodity is increased while all other inputs are held fixed, a point will eventually be reached at which additions yield progressively smaller, or finishing, increases in output" (The Editors of Encyclopedia Britannica, 2021).

What this basically boils down to is that although you can reach a certain point in something that you practice, if the bar isn't raised gradually after a certain amount of time, what you are doing is always in danger of becoming stagnant. What you need to take from this is that however high you get your WPM, if you do not keep up the practice and try to improve as time goes on, your thought process will become a little labored on the subject and a sort of internal boredom will settle. Keeping our brain and ourselves in general on our toes is always fundamental in self-improvement, and speed-reading is no different.

Now that you have come this far, you are really starting to make progress in your journey. I hope that what you are learning is opening your mind to the possibilities of speed-reading as a whole and understanding that it is not the Everest that you first assumed it to be.

Sometimes, when I think back to that scared child shaking in front of his classmates with a copy of *Lord of the Flies* in his sweaty hand, I have to smile at how far I have come in terms of my WPM and my unwavering love of literature. If someone had told me back then that I would be reading at the rate that I am today, I would have laughed them out of the building.

However, that was just my mindset and the mindset of thousands of others who, like me, had just been taught reading techniques that did not suit them. Maybe you were the same, or maybe you just feel that your speed and comprehension could be improved. Whatever the case may be, you have come to the right place, and I am really glad that you have joined me on this journey. If you are currently practicing the steps we have been through, then a big cheer for you, as you are well on your way.

In the next chapter, we will learn how to not only comprehend but make it last in our memory for the long haul. Keep on reading and remember that you are doing brilliantly so far. Just keep that practice up and concentrate on all of the positives it brings.

Chapter 6

Remember Not to Forget

We have all been there. You finish a chapter, look up from the book, and realize that absolutely nothing went in. There are many reasons why this happens. It can just be the text itself is not engaging our own personal tastes, or we have not set ourselves up in the correct manner. Distractions, reading pace, technique and any number of variables can affect the way we read and the comprehension of the text.

In this chapter, we will look at some techniques and tips to help you improve your study and also your enjoyment of leisurely reading. Many of the things that we will discuss will only involve small adjustments, yet they will yield massive results. Much like the previous techniques in the book, practice will make perfect, so try to stick with them when you implement them into your daily routine.

Study, as a skill, is vitally important, so if you are learning speed-reading to help you improve, then you will need to have dedication to the process. As you begin to see improvements in your speed-reading, the productivity of your study will also improve. Try to take everything on board here and keep up your training, as going into this thing halfway does not work, and your full attention is needed. I am certain that you are aware of this, and you are ready to give it everything you have.

Our brain takes in information 24/7. Even as we sleep, our subconscious is recycling everything that we have seen or heard throughout the day and filing away what we need and what can be disposed of. With everything that goes into our mind throughout the days, weeks, months, and years, it is no wonder that a lot of it slips through the net. This is a good thing because if everything was to stick, then we would be completely overwhelmed with information, memories, and images. It is healthy for our brain to let go of the things that we do not need, but we must keep training it to hold on to the ones we need.

Accessing and applying the full potential of the mind can open an endless amount of doors in our lives, and further methods and techniques of how to set and achieve outstanding goals, build your memory recall and greatly improve your productivity are discussed in my book, *How to Learn Faster and Be More Productive,* but for now, we are going to concentrate on your WPM and your intake of literature.

Our sensory memory—what we see, hear and touch—always has to pass through the filter of our short-term memory first. What this means is that our short-term memory is the first part of our brain to access all of the information we consume during the day. What happens here is a sort of filtering, where the memories that we are about to sort go into our working memory, which in general, can last up to 70–80 minutes, depending on interest and severity of the sense experienced (Frost, 2016).

Once our thoughts and senses are passed into our working memory, we need to give it a reason to stick around. If we want this information to remain in our long-term memory, then we must stop from time to time and think about what we have just read. This can be vital in making the memories stick, and there are several techniques to do this that we will discuss throughout this chapter.

Strong emotions will of course stick around longer without much of an effort on our part. Times that we were hurt or scored the winning touchdown when we were kids will always have a more permanent place in our long-term memory.

Oftentimes, a song we hear on a playlist or at a party that we hadn't thought of in years will evoke strong, sometimes overwhelming memories that we had presumed lost forever. Yet, when they come back with such force, we are struck by the sheer severity of them. This was our brain storing them side-by-side with a memory jogger. Many people use a form of this as a tactic for study, and it is a great way of remembering through association.

I mention this only to show you that there are ways of remembering many things that we never really thought we could; many times, the memories that we believed were gone forever have actually been stored away and are actually in near-mint condition. The only problem is that we never learned how to access them. Once we learn the correct way to process them in the techniques to come, then pulling them out when needed will become a whole lot easier.

Many times, the issue is in how your mindset was going into reading. If you approach it in a passive manner, then of course the information will only briefly stick around, and if you are lucky, maybe two or three points will remain prevalent a little bit longer. This sort of passive reading can occur for many reasons, with the main ones being your interest in the text and your technique.

Throughout life, there will be forms of literature we have to consume which holds little or no interest to us. Maybe it is for a thesis in the one subject that you hate but need the grades in, or maybe it is a project in work that you got dragged into but find extremely boring. Whatever the case may be, you will need the information to stick to benefit from the situation.

During these times, you will need to approach the text in a very active manner. Concentrate and take a moment after each paragraph or section to let the information sink in. Question what you have read and try to challenge yourself in remembering the significant words and points.

The physical act of writing down the points that you are finding most challenging will help in making the information pass into your long-term memory. Not only that, it will be easier to check back over it when you need to access it. However, this is only to be used when studying extensive or extremely challenging text.

What you will need to aim for now that you have finished reading the text is get to a point where you fully believe that you will be able to recite the information in your own words. Try and imagine that you now have to teach it to someone else who has no prior knowledge on the subject. Would you be able to inform them sufficiently enough that they would be educated on the matter?

Before you begin any form of study, you need to be relaxed. Even though we are practicing speed-reading here, that does not mean you can leave it all until the last minute and then hammer everything home on the way to an exam. When we pile pressure on ourselves, our minds will be so preoccupied with worry that the studying of the text will become irrelevant. Find yourself some alone time, and take a few breaths before you begin. Making yourself as comfortable as possible will go a long way to putting you in a position where you are fully ready to learn.

Remember what we mentioned earlier in the book: If you are studying something of importance, the tip is not to speed read three different books on the subject but to repeat the process three times on the same text. This way the information has a much greater chance of being retained in your long-term memory.

Always recap and summarize. This can be done at the end of each chapter, or even each section if the text is heavily information-based writing. You do not have to read back over it each time, but you will need to take a moment and ask yourself some questions regarding the things that you have just learned. Try and ask the questions that you would be most worried about being asked in a test. This way, you are instinctively storing the information you found most challenging.

This is called Pause and Recall, and it can be done in three simple steps. We have briefly touched on them already, but I will lay them out for you here:

- When finishing a paragraph, stop for a moment and let it sink in.

- If you come to an important point or phrase in the middle of a paragraph, stop regardless and let that stick.

- Do the same at the end of each chapter.

Now, I know this step sounds fairly obvious, but try and recall the last time you really did this while reading. How often have we just "plowed through" and hoped that the information would stick? This technique should be used for most texts that need attention, but if what you are studying is of vital importance, then taking notes may also be a good idea.

Another effective technique that some people use is to think in pictures. This method works especially well for visual learners, whose brains process images far more efficiently than words or numbers, but it can apply to anyone. What you need to do is to make a note of any keywords that you spot during your reading (using a highlighter pen here is helpful) and visualize them as an image.

Once the images are stored in your mind, the particular words will be a lot easier to access, and the information that goes along with them will be there, too. Memorizing headings and subheadings in this way can be extremely productive too, as the whole structure of the text will be firmly set in your mind, and recalling the keywords and notes that you made will be a whole lot easier.

One of the things that I find extremely helpful is thinking in analogies. This involves taking a piece of text or information that I find particularly tedious and associating it with something I find interesting. When we do this, we take away a lot of the stigma attached to a section of a book or a study that only seems to result in making our minds go blank.

If what you are reading is on the "Positive and Negative Effects of Quantum Physics Concerning Matter Transportation," and the idea of trying to make the information stick is giving you sleepless nights, then try to connect the main points to another subject or interest that you enjoy. Linking all of the parts to a different, yet similar in structure, piece of information will allow you to access the information on your terms.

What I mean by this is that when we link information with another memory or subject that we are already well versed in, we place it in our long-term memory alongside something that is easily accessible. Pulling out the information that we want will not only be easier, but it will also be a lot easier to explain both to ourselves and others.

All of these tips, when applied to speed-reading, become a huge part of how we will study in the years ahead. The techniques that we have already been practicing to improve our WPM and our comprehension go hand in hand with the ideas in this chapter. Once they are implemented together, then the information that we are trying to keep in our long-term memory will be easier to retain and recall later.

When using these techniques while reading for leisure, the visualization step I mentioned earlier is a wonderful way to enjoy the experience. When we read a fiction novel, a good author will try to help us to do this with how they choose their words and paint their imagery, so implementing this technique at times like this is a lot easier than a scientific text or business memo, so try to enjoy it.

You must also take a moment to absorb the information at times when you are reading for pleasure because as much as you are enjoying what you are doing, some of the plot points will still slip by and end up ruining your enjoyment if you are not keeping up your general speed-reading practice. Making sure that you are letting all of the information stick is not only helping with this practice as you go, it is also massively improving your reading pleasure.

What you should never do is start a book and not finish it. Even if it is not the most gripping of reads, you should always see it through. Regardless of the text that is being consumed, dropping a book a few pages in because it doesn't blow you away will become a habit, and allowing yourself to build any quitting mentality is never a good idea.

Oftentimes, practicing speed-reading with literature that isn't quite to your fancy is actually more productive in the long run, as we have to concentrate a lot harder on getting the information to stick. This is not to say that everything you read should be mundane, but if you start a James Patterson novel, then what did you expect? In all seriousness, you need to stick with it, as everything that goes in, whether we want to retain the information or not, is all a part of training your brain. When you train your brain with a positive information overload, you should think of it like working out a muscle.

Let us recap some of the tips and tricks that we have discussed in this chapter. Remember to not just implement them to the level of the text that you are reading but to always be aware of what you are studying:

- Pause and recall: Take the time to ingest what you have read.

- Relax: Do not try and cram everything into your mind an hour before a big exam.

- Read three times: When the text is of high importance, do not speed-read three different books. Read the same one three times.

- Recap and summarize: Ask yourself what occurred in the text you have read to help it stick.

- Think in pictures: Add images in your mind that relate to the keywords. This is especially useful with fiction.

- Link to analogies: Tie the tougher information together with something that you are passionate and knowledgeable about.

- Practice: Even when reading for pleasure, stick to your techniques at all times.

This last one is so important. Any life skill will become diminished if we do not maintain the high standards that we originally set. As I have said many times, letting your practice slip will always bring you back to the point where you started, as skill is built and maintained with consistent quality practice. Even when you reach a point where you have far surpassed what you had originally set out to achieve, you must continue to work at the techniques that we have been through. This I am sure you are doing and will continue to do, and I only reinforce the point to help you along on your journey.

Remember that you are doing brilliantly so far, and if you have already got your WPM up from where it began, then I applaud you. If the speed that you are after is taking a little longer to achieve than you had hoped, please don't be disheartened, as you will get there if you keep it up. It is only a matter of time.

In the next chapter, we will bring it all home with some last-minute tips to help you fine-tune the already purring machine that is your speed-reading. I will reinforce some of the most important points that we have covered and sprinkle them with a few more positives that you can apply and negatives that can be removed from your reading process respectively. Keep on reading and practicing because you are on the homestretch now, and we have come a long way together already.

Chapter 7

Some Last Minute Tips

We may be coming near the end of the book, but your training has only really begun, as practicing the techniques that you have learned is an ongoing process. As we have mentioned, even if you get to a place that you deem adequate, neglecting the things that you have learned and letting them become rusty will result in your standards slipping.

Everything that we have been through together is designed to improve your intake of information and strengthen your brain in the process. Keeping it challenged will become a part of your daily routine, and anything that improves our well-being is a marvelous gift that should be treasured and treated with the utmost care.

Of course, when you reach your desired WPM, the training does not have to be as intense, and bringing it down to once or twice a week should be sufficient. All of this will be discussed in a little more detail later in this chapter when we go back over the techniques and tips and lay them all out beside each other.

The steps and techniques that we have been through may seem vast when they are spread out over several pages like this, but so many of them become one when they are properly used. What you need to remember is that once you first start your training, there may only seem to be a slight improvement at the beginning, but that is perfectly natural. The longer that you stick to it and the more work you put in, the faster the results will come.

This is why it is so important to try and concentrate on the positives. Even if you only bring your WPM up by a perceived small amount, it still went up. If you can only manage to bring your borders in by one word on each side at the beginning of your perceptual expansion training, then at least you have that, and you know the rest will come. Specialist skills do not come easily, and if they did, then they wouldn't be termed "specialist."

Before we get into revising our techniques, let us just quickly go over the things that you should avoid doing when trying to improve your speed-reading. Although most of what you are practicing is designed to eliminate these little errors, it is never a bad thing to reinforce them so we can concentrate on what makes our reading experience as productive and enjoyable as it can be.

Stop Your Inner Monologue

This is a big one, and it is a very hard habit to break. Since we first learned to read, we have been taught to sound the words out in our mind as we scan the text. This subvocalization not only slows us down, but it encourages us to take every word as one. As we learned in the third chapter, "Slow Is Smooth, Smooth Is Fast," this will cause us to backtrack on each word as our brain tries to help us make a complete sentence. However, we can take each sentence—or at least large chunks of it—as a whole.

Our inner monologue will always be there, of course, but it will only be ingesting the text that is needed. Each single word will just become a part of the whole sentence, which is where all of the information that we need is contained anyhow. When we see the words, "I love you," written at the end of a letter or a text message, we do not subvocalize each word because it is such a common phrase. Once you begin to master eliminating your inner monologue to the point where it is only processing what you need, then most sentences will be taken in this way.

As you begin to master the techniques and your speed-reading improves, the pace at which you are moving will naturally help you with controlling your inner monologue. The steps used in perfecting your WPM are built to do just this, and if you are practicing on a daily basis early on, then you may not even notice as this habit of subvocalization begins to fade.

Do Not Reread

We have mentioned this a few times as it is so important, but going back over text while you are in your flow will not just slow you down, it will make it very hard to find your rhythm again. Perfecting your speed-reading is as much about believing in your ability to have absorbed the information as it is about practicing the techniques. Far too often, it can feel very tempting to skip back and make sure that we read a name or a keyword correctly, but if it is either of these things or anything else important, then it will most certainly have been processed.

Try and remember that if the literature you are reading is heavily fact-based text or an important study, you will be giving it another read or two again at your new and improved pace, as we have covered earlier in the book. This I firmly recommend, as absorbing these kinds of texts will take a lot more effort and control. What we are talking about here applies more to fiction or reading for pleasure, although the general principles are exactly the same. If it is important information, then you still should not stop to backtrack because even if you missed something, you would definitely get it the next time.

It is not only our rhythm and flow that are affected by rereading. Our enjoyment and comprehension are also heavily influenced when we keep stopping to check back. This may take some getting used to, but as time goes on and your practice really starts to take hold, then the need to stop and look back over what you have read will become a lot easier to resist.

Find Alone Time to Practice

Distraction is probably the biggest hindrance to your speed-reading progression, especially in the beginning. When you first begin your training, always make sure that you have rid yourself of any opportunities to become preoccupied. Switch your phone off, put the kids to bed, or wait until you have the house to yourself. Whatever you need to do to get some peace and quiet will be vitally important.

When we allow things to distract us from doing anything concerning our mind and concentration, then it will be extremely difficult to get the results we desire. There is no grey area here, it is just a fact that reading, and especially speed-reading, does not work well when we are not giving it our full attention.

Once you have begun to reach a higher standard and a much better WPM, then doing so while there are things going on around you will certainly become easier, but until then, your full attention will be needed. Finding a little alone time and making yourself comfortable is essential if you want to progress productively.

Now that we have touched on the negative habits that can affect our speed-reading progress, let us run back through the positives. Some of these are techniques that we have mentioned you are practicing already, and a few will be little tips for you to add to your arsenal. Each and every one of them are as important as the next, so you will have to give each of them your undivided attention and dedication, which I am sure you have been doing the whole way through.

Never Give Up

There will be times when you may think that just going back to the way things were will seem like the more attractive option. Please do everything you can to fight this impulse. Of course, dropping something hard always seems easier at the time compared to seeing it out, but has anyone ever felt good about themselves when they do?

Digging in and fighting for something that seems so tough at times is what makes us human. The best things in life may be free, but they will come to you with effort, and mastering speed-reading is no different. Trust me, I speak from experience here. When I think back to the kid in front of his classmates struggling to string two words together, I will always give myself a pat on the back for getting to where I am today.

Why? We must be proud of our accomplishments at all times. Doing so is not arrogant or selfish, it is just something that we have to do because at the end of the day, the only opinion that matters is our own. If you can look in the mirror each evening and tell yourself that you gave it your all, then there is no more to be said, so you need to celebrate the effort that you have made.

Give *this* your all, and the results will continue to grow. When you reach your target WPM, you can always drop the daily training and reduce it slightly to suit your weekly routine. However, it is important to polish your new skill and to always come back to it. Maintaining and constantly improving what you have learned is fundamental.

Regularly Calculate Your WPM

This is why we are here. When you start your speed-reading journey you, of course, must first find out your WPM. Remember to be honest with yourself when calculating this. Follow the steps from Chapter 3 and write down the number on a piece of paper. This number is important, so keep it safe. You will need it to measure your newer scores against, and it will also be a reminder in the months and years that follow of how far you have really come. Tracking and seeing your progress will help you to stay motivated and you will then put more into your training.

Building and improving a skill is fulfilling and rewarding, and when working toward any goal, you have to stay focused, dedicate yourself, and give one hundred percent effort. Anything less will only bring results that you will never be fully satisfied with, and at the end of the day, all you are doing for your training is reading, and we all know how much we love to read.

The Meta Guiding Technique

Using a finger, a pen, or a playing card to run along the text may seem childish to some, but this is only because of our conditioned view of reading as a whole; the truth of the matter is that it is a much more productive way to absorb the text than flicking our eyes back and forth with nothing to guide them, so grab that marker and get to reading.

Although you have all of the information on how to speed-read in these pages, you will also have this section to use as a brief summary of all of the techniques and tips that you need to keep up with your practice. Having them all in one place will make it a lot easier to access them, and it will save you time on your actual training, which is what is important right now.

The Meta Guiding technique is probably the most tried and tested technique in speed-reading, and it has always shown amazing results. When we use a marker, we massively eliminate the option of backtracking, and as we know from the "Stop Your Inner Monologue" section in this chapter, going back over the text is a huge hindrance. When we run our finger or a pen along the line of words, our vision completely focuses on only moving forward.

Remember to take a quick moment at the end of each paragraph or section to let the information sink in. Just flicking your eyes away from the page for a second should suffice. It will be ample time to give your brain a chance to reboot, and your eyes will be all the better for the break from all of the quick movement. These are all of the small things that, when they are combined, become one speed-reading component, and when we add them all up, makes all of the techniques work together.

Use Your Borders

Training your perceptual expansion will increase your WPM drastically. As we discussed in Chapter 4, your peripheral vision has always been active, it is only a matter of acknowledging it and allowing it to become part of your reading experience.

Drawing your imaginary borders on each side of the page will be tough at first, but with plenty of practice, you will soon be visualizing those guidelines as soon as you open a book and then putting the technique into action automatically. Remember to start small at first and work your way in. Trying to overdo it at the beginning is likely to leave you disheartened and will actually end up slowing you down due to you constantly missing information and backtracking.

When you combine this method with using your marker, the tiring effect of your saccadic eye movement will also be greatly reduced, and this stops you from tiring as quickly. All of this combines to help your speed-reading to improve and your comprehension to be more effective.

Set Your Reading Goals and Stick to Them

Set yourself daily and weekly goals to aim for in your speed-reading training. Do not set them too high at the beginning: keep them realistic but not easy. It is important to push yourself toward something that is achievable to keep you motivated. Remember to up them as the weeks go by, and keep testing yourself to beat your score from the previous week. There is nothing wrong with trying to better yourself, and when it comes to something as important as reading and the quest for knowledge, then we really need to give it our all, don't we?

This is not about punishing yourself when you do not hit your targets, it is about rewarding yourself when you do. Letting ourselves get hung up on our perceived failures is what makes us human, but we need to shake that feeling off right now because perfecting this thing is tough but worth the effort. If you practice as hard as you can, then you will get there. Just try not to be too hard on yourself if you get the same score a few times in a row. I firmly believe that the carrot works better than the stick in this case.

Once you have your weekly planner done and broken it down into a daily routine, make sure that you stick to it. This is more important than bettering your score each time, as this is a marathon and not a sprint. Each time that you follow the techniques that you have learned and apply them to any text, you are improving as a speed-reader. There is no secret here; practice makes perfect in any walk of life, and this is no different.

Chunking

We briefly touched on this earlier, but we will bring it home here. When we apply "chunking" to our reading, we train ourselves to take several words together at once. This is not really a separate skill or tip, as such, but more so an added bonus that will occur naturally to you as the other techniques manifest themselves in your daily reading routine.

You will begin to see its effects as time goes by. Oftentimes, when it becomes a part of your reading skill set, you may not have even noticed that you had started to do it. The beauty of the main techniques that you have learned and are practicing right now is that so many of the components you need to master this will be given to you as you progress. Being able to "chunk" several words together as you pass rapidly over them is just another one of these.

Keep Reading

This is pretty self-explanatory, but you would be surprised at how many people let it slip. Reading is a gift, and although some of you are here because you want to improve your WPM for work or study, which is very admirable, every one of us enjoys a good book, so you must keep reading.

It does not have to take over your life, but if you can constantly have a novel or even a well-written magazine on your bedside table, then you will be on the right path. Not every book that we pick up is going to be one that grips us, but as long as you are consuming some form of literature even for a few minutes each day, then you will be sure of a constant improvement.

By reading as little as 10 pages each day, you will amazingly still finish around 15–20 books a year. It is all about dedication and sticking to a task. Every book that you finish will be an achievement, and if you ever feel that you can skip a day or that reading is becoming tedious, try and remember what Mark Twain said: "The man who does not read has no advantage over the man who cannot read them" (Quote Investigator, 2011).

Keep Learning

Broadening our vocabulary is an important tool in speed-reading. The more words that we understand, the less need for us to backtrack and lose our flow. Oftentimes, we will stumble upon words that we are unsure of, but you have to keep your rhythm and look them up later if you must.

Knowledge is so important in helping us grow. If you are not learning, then you are standing still, and nothing good was ever achieved this way. When we stimulate our mind we are helping ourselves in wonderful ways. The more information that we absorb, the more confident we feel. Once you have really started to perfect your training, then this world will be much easier to access, and the text that you are reading will be comprehended in a far superior manner.

As our practice really takes hold and our brain is being properly challenged by us every time we pick up a book, learning in our daily lives will become a whole lot easier. This is because the speed-reading we are practicing stimulates our brain in so many different ways and the things that we hear and see throughout the day will be retained and dismissed a lot more sufficiently.

When you read a book, especially a well-written one, you are accessing the skills, knowledge, research, and know-how that the author has collected, tested, and perfected through their lives. The real beauty is that they have condensed it down into one manuscript that you can hold in your hand. When you add in your speed-reading and apply it to the text, you will then be in a position to consume and retain it all within a very short space of time. I see that as a real privilege.

Sending You on Your Way

Warren Buffett, the billionaire investor, entrepreneur, philanthropist, and business magnate reportedly reads 500 pages a day. He claims that much of his success is owed to his love of all things literature, believing that the stimulation that he gives his brain each day opens his mind up to deal with everything else that life throws at him (Quote Investigator, 2018).

Buffett says, "Read 500 pages like this every day. This is how knowledge works. It builds up like compound interest" (Quote Investigator, 2018). Now, we can't all devour 500 hundred pages a day, but what we can do is give it our best shot. Much like setting goals in your training, you do not need to set yours at Warren Buffett's daily amount! All you have to do is aim a little higher each time. You never know: Maybe one day, through heavy practice, you will reach the sort of numbers he does. For now though, you only need to concentrate on your targets.

The average amount of books a top CEO will read is around the 60 per year mark. That boils down to roughly five a month. This again may feel like a high number, but for many people, it is highly achievable. We want to read as much as we can, I think we can take that as a given, but setting your goals too high at the beginning may break your spirit a little when you are not hitting Buffett-esque standards in the first week. Remember that we are only concentrating on the wins here, so try and only use the times that you do not hit your target as a motivational tool and not a stick to beat yourself with.

Before we come to our conclusion, I want you to give yourself a moment (Look up from the page for a second to let the information stick!) and congratulate yourself. Be proud that you not only made a decision to better your reading but that you have stuck it out all this way. Far too often in life, it is a much easier option to just say, "This is not for me," but when we see something out to the end, then the results are almost exclusively positive.

Try and remind yourself that knowing something and taking action are two completely different things. Making slight improvements and understanding the techniques isn't enough. Only through constant practice over time will you find the results that you desire.

I hope that what you have learned will not only help you to achieve your target but will also help to banish any painful memories, like standing in front of a class like I did with a tattered copy of William Golding's classic in my shaking hand, and you will become the type of reader who is proud of the standards they have set. I can promise that if you stick to your practice and give it the attention and dedication that it deserves, then the results you seek are only a matter of time away.

Conclusion

In the introduction to this book and the beginning of our journey together, I alluded to the large novel that has sat on your bookshelf looking like Everest. Well, now that your training is beginning to take hold, that copy of *The Lord of the Rings*, or whatever your mountain may be, is hopefully starting to not only look like a manageable trek but the type of excursion you are now certain that you will enjoy.

I am certain that when Evelyn Wood first started her "Dynamics Reading" business in the late 1950s, she could never have imagined that it would take off the way it did ("Evelyn Wood (teacher)," 2020). Not only that, but I also wonder if she grasped how much it would help people like myself to overcome their fear of the written word and become voracious readers.

Although her training and techniques differed from the more advanced ones that I have presented to you in these pages, the basic principles are very alike. All that has been done to improve them is to take an already good process and iron out the creases a little. Through my own experiences, I have been able to remove what are (in my opinion) the nonessentials and replace them with tried and tested techniques that I have found to be the fastest to learn, the easiest to practice and that have worked the best in my experience.

Productivity is a staple of my life, and I like things to be completed to the best possible standard. This is what we should always apply to everything that we do, especially when it concerns self-improvement and our general well-being. Why should we settle for anything less than the best of our ability?

As I have stated, being able to broaden your mind at speed is a great tool to have where reading is concerned. Having the chance to learn a new skill, study faster, and expand your knowledge gives you a massive advantage. Another positive is that giving your brain a good workout has been proven to vastly improve sleep among so many other things. When we have given our mind sufficient sustenance throughout the day, relaxing at the end of it all becomes a whole lot easier.

Practice, evaluate, and achieve. These are the three main points that you should apply to your newly learned techniques. Do this, and the results that you have dreamt of are just around the corner. Sure, there will be days when your mind gets tired or it seems like you are pushing a boulder up a hill, but these days will be few and far between, and the general feeling of accomplishment will far outweigh the negativity that will try to sneak in from time to time.

Practicing for something like speed-reading is not the tedious exercise that it is with so many other goals in life because the results come relatively fast. When we really think about it, reading is a pleasurable experience. I know that it may not have been something that you have enjoyed up until this point, that is probably why you are here, but once you have shaken off the stigma and fear that it had once represented to you, your love for everything literature will grow. Like everything that you love, you will begin to wonder how you ever lived without it.

Whenever your evaluation process does not yield the results that you were hoping for, please do not despair—they will be better the next time or the one after that. If you stick to your practice, then the results can only improve as time goes by, and all that has happened is that you most probably set your targets just a little too high compared to the amount of time that you were able to set aside for practice at first.

There is nothing wrong with this—it only means that you are an ambitious person, which is a fantastic trait to have. If you are ambitious, then I am sure that you are also determined and dedicated, so the results that you want in the long run will certainly be achieved.

That is the ultimate goal, isn't it? To *achieve*. When we get something in life that we have worked for, it always feels a million times better than when something is just handed to us. This is because we are ambitious beings by nature, and wanting to be the best that we can be at something is ingrained in us. Getting to that point in any challenge where we are sure that we have beaten or mastered it is a wonderful moment, and although speed-reading is an ongoing practice, the goals that you wish to achieve will be reached, and the only reason that you will keep at it is to maintain your standards and then surpass what you set out to do.

Speed-reading is one of life's greatest tools when it is used to its full potential. I can wholeheartedly attest to that. When it is applied to our lives in a positive way, it can vastly improve our productivity in almost everything that we do. From freeing up our time to do other things, to helping with our comprehension of the test that we have just studied. The possibilities are endless.

Take a look at that bookshelf in the corner of the room and all of the endless tales that sit upon it. As you progress in your training and the techniques and tips that I have laid down for you begin to take hold, all of the literature and enjoyment in those pages will become yours for the taking. This is something that I am passionate about because reading is a gift, and no one should be held back from it.

You have done so well to get to this point, and the hardest part is out of the way. I have tried to really bring home the importance of practice throughout this book, but I have also been very insistent on giving yourself a break. That is why understanding that the hardest work that you have to do is out of the way if you have completed the tasks that have been put forth.

All I want to finish with is to give you one last hearty pat on the back because what you have achieved thus far is no small feat. If you hit a roadblock at any stage, just remind yourself of why you came here in the first place and the energy to push on will come. I hope that you will continue what you have started and that all of the literature in the world will open up to you as it did for me.

Before we leave each other for now, I would like to thank you for having read my book. I know the fears, worry and frustrations attached to reading all too well, but I also know the pride and joy that it can bring when approached with the right mindset and with the correct tools. You have those tools now—all you need to do is keep them sharp, keep moving forwards and to keep picking up those books.

Best wishes for all your future successes.

Thanks for Reading

I just wanted to say thank you for taking the time to read through my book. I am truly grateful.

If you have found my book helpful, and if you have a few spare moments, I'd really appreciate you leaving me a review.

Please scan the appropriate QR code below with you cell phone camera or visit Amazon to leave a:

US Review   **UK Review**

Wishing you success in all your future endeavors.

Joseph Milano

- Joseph

References

Akhan, A. (2016, December 29). *How to Speed Read a Business Book in 90 Minutes | Scoro.* Scoro.com. https://www.scoro.com/blog/how-to-speed-read-a-business-book/

Al. (2019, July 20). *How to Remember What You Read (9 Actionable Tips).* Improveism. https://improveism.com/remember-what-you-read/

Blake, G. (n.d.). *Reading Speed Calculation formula.* LSAT Hacks. https://lsathacks.com/lsat-courses/lsat-reading-comprehension-course/reading-speed-calculator/

Bullard, A. (2015, March 17). *How to Read Faster: 10 Ways to Increase Your Reading Speed.* Lifehack. https://www.lifehack.org/articles/productivity/10-ways-increase-your-reading-speed.html

Evelyn Wood (teacher). (2020, December 15). In *Wikipedia.* https://en.wikipedia.org/wiki/Evelyn_Wood_(teacher)

Ferriss, T. (2009, July 31). *Scientific Speed Reading: How to Read 300% Faster in 20 Minutes.* The Blog of Author Tim

Ferriss. https://tim.blog/2009/07/30/speed-reading-and-accelerated-learning/

Frost, R. (2016, January 12). Why do we forget 99% of what we read? [Blog comment]. Quora. Retrieved from https://www.quora.com/Why-do-we-forget-99-of-what-we-read

Goldentouch, L., & PhD. (2015, May 2). *Meta Guiding*. Key to Study. https://www.keytostudy.com/metaguiding/

Klemm, B. (2014, July 17). *How to improve memory skills and remember what you read: Beyond phonics and "whole language.* SharpBrains. https://sharpbrains.com/blog/2014/07/17/how-to-improve-memory-skills-and-remember-what-you-read-beyond-phonics-and-whole-language/

Masters, D. (2016, March 21). *If you're not assessing then you're guessing!* Masters Fitness. https://mastersfitness.co.uk/not-assessing-then-youre-guessing/

Mind Tools Content Team. (2009). *Speed Reading: – How to Absorb Information Quickly and Effectively*. Mindtools.com. https://www.mindtools.com/speedrd.html

Purves, D., Augustine, G. J., Fitzpatrick, D., Katz, L. C., LaMantia, A.-S., McNamara, J. O., & S Mark Williams. (2016). *Types of Eye Movements and Their Functions*. Nih.gov; Sinauer Associates https://www.ncbi.nlm.nih.gov/books/NBK10991/

Quote Investigator. (2011, December 11) *The Man Who Does Not Read Has No Advantage Over The Man Who Cannot Read*. Quote Investigator.

https://quoteinvestigator.com/2012/12/11/cannot
-read

Quote Investigator. (2018, October 20). *Read 500 Pages Like This Every Day. That's How Knowledge Works. It Builds Up, Like Compound Interest.* Quote Investigator. https://quoteinvestigator.com/2018/10/20/pages/ *Speed Reading.* (2021, June 16). In *Wikipedia.* https://en.wikipedia.org/wiki/Speed_reading

Rayner, K., Schotter, E. R., Masson, M. E. J., Potter, M. C., & Treiman, R. (2016). *Psychological Science in the Public Interest*, 17(1), 4–34. Much to Read, So Little Time. https://doi.org/10.1177/1529100615623267

Speed Reading. (2019, April 9). *Reading Speed Calculation Formula.* Speed Reading App. https://speedreadings.com/reading-speed-calculation/

The Editors of Encyclopedia Britannica. (2017). *diminishing returns | Definition & Example.* Encyclopedia Britannica.com. https://www.britannica.com/topic/diminishing-returns

Train your brain. (2021, February 15). *Train your brain.* Harvard Health Publishing. https://www.health.harvard.edu/mind-and-mood/train-your-brain

Yu, D., Legge, G. E., Wagoner, G., & Chung, S. T. (2018). Training peripheral vision to read: Boosting the speed of letter processing. *Vision research*, *152*, 51-60.

Printed in Great Britain
by Amazon